Prairie Wildflowers

Showy Wildflowers of the Plains, Valleys, and Foothills in the Northern Rocky Mountain States.

photography and text by
Dr. Dee Strickler

illustration and graphic design by
Zoe Strickler-Wilson

Front Cover: Primrose Family *(Primulaceae)*

PRAIRIE SHOOTING STAR

Dodecatheon conjugens Greene.
Shooting Stars or Bird Bills have
singular reflexed petals that bring ins-
tant recognition. The gorgeous shades
of pink or magenta of the petals and
the yellow and black stamens produce
a stunning floral display. Smooth bright
green leaves cluster at the base of the
plant and the bare flower stems are
smooth and unbranched. Look for
shooting stars in the spring. HABITAT:
Prairies and meadows on fairly deep
soil where moist in the spring. RANGE:
B.C. and Alberta to Wyoming and
California, east of the Cascade summit.
COMMENT: We have two species of
Dodecatheon on our prairies and
several others in the mountains.

Library of Congress Catalog Card 86-90566
ISBN 0-934318-99-9

Published by The Flower Press
Columbia Falls, Montana

Publishing Consultant:
Falcon Press Publishing Co., Inc.,
Helena and Billings, Montana

To order extra copies of this book, contact:

The Flower Press, 192 Larch Lane, Columbia Falls, MT·59912, or

Falcon Press, P.O. Box 279, Billings, MT 59103 or call toll-free
1-800-582-BOOK (outside Montana) or 1-800-592-BOOK (in
Montana).

Printed in Singapore.

Acknowledgements

In the preparation of this book the author owes a debt of gratitude to numerous people for help in plant identification, proof reading and other assistance. Special thanks and appreciation are extended to Dr. Jeanette Oliver, botanist at Flathead Valley Community College, Kalispell, Montana, for help in identifying difficult species and editing the manuscript. Many of the flowers pictured have been pressed, dried and deposited in the herbarium of FVCC.

I wish also to recognize the kind assistance of Drs. Adolph Hecht, Amy Gilmartin and Joy Mastroguiseppe of Washington State University, Dr. Kathleen Peterson and Jeffrey Strachan of the University of Montana and Dr. Burrell Nelson of the University of Wyoming.

My daughter Zoe Strickler-Wilson contributed substantially with constructive criticism as well as supplying the graphic design and art work.

Finally special thanks go to Claire, my wife and frequent hiking companion, for help with the manuscript and for constant support and encouragement. To her this book is dedicated.

—Whitefish, Montana. July, 1986

About the author

Dee Strickler is a Wood Scientist and Technologist holding a B.S. from Washington State University, M.S. from Syracuse University and a Doctorate from Duke University. His Forestry undergraduate curriculum included a minor in Botany. As Wood Technologist on the College of Engineering Faculty of Washington State University for many years, he authored over 50 technical publications and reports on original research in the fields of wood properties and glued wood products.

Dr. Strickler has enjoyed wildflower photography for more than 20 years and herein shares that interest and enjoyment with others.

Contents

Introduction

PRAIRIE WILDFLOWERS is the first of a three volume series on the flowering plants of the Northern Rocky Mountain States. FOREST WILDFLOWERS, Part II of this series, includes the flowers of woods, forests and mountains in the Northern Rockies. ALPINE WILDFLOWERS completes the series.

These guidebooks will help hikers, outdoorsmen, travelers, amateur botanists and all lovers of nature who want to know "What flower is that?" Professional botanists and range managers will find them a useful supplement to more authoritative works on the flora of the Northern Rockies. School teachers and students from elementary schools to universities will also use them as beginner's guides to botany and wildflower appreciation.

The flowers in this book appear in family sequence. The system of grouping flowers by color is not used, because wide color variations frequently occur within a single species. Page 13 shows a good example of color differences in Sego Lily.

For each flower pictured, some of the most noticeable features of the species are described, including the leaves, blooming period, habitat and range in which the plant grows. Some pertinent comments of general interest about the species or the family usually conclude the discussion.

The flowers shown in this or any similar guide can only include a sample of the seemingly endless array in our natural world. The comments pertaining to individual flowers in the text frequently mention other closely related species that one may encounter. An attempt was made to include at least one species from each family and each major genus of showy wildflowers commonly found in the prairie flora of the Northern Rockies. This was not always possible, especially in the case of the Sunflower Family, which is represented in the Northwest by approximately 100 genera and nearly 1,000 species. In the interest of space some common lawn and garden pests were omitted, as well as plants used in agriculture and small inconspicuous flowers. Thus one will not find the common dandelion, alfalfa or sweet clover in this work.

Some agricultural pests are included, that may not be readily recognized by many people. Furthermore a beautiful wildflower to one person may represent a noxious weed to another. The author hopes that a fair balance has been achieved and that everyone can discover beauty and pleasure among these pages.

Page 8 has a map showing the general range of most of the prairie wildflowers pictured in this book.

Protected natural areas offer the best opportunities for wildflower enthusiasts to explore freely for wildflowers and other natural delights. These include both State and National Parks, Monuments, Wildlife Refuges, National Grasslands and the many National and State Forests. In addition, a huge portion of our prairie land is in federal ownership under the control of the Bureau of Land Management. Virtually all of it is leased for grazing of livestock or other commercial purposes. Maps of BLM lands and National Forests can be obtained from those agencies for a nominal fee.

Prairie Wildflowers

"Prairie" as used in this book includes desert, plains, open valleys and foothills from low to near subalpine terrain.

Selection of those flowers to be included under prairie species was based on whether or not the plants commonly grow in wide open spaces below timberline. Some plants may be found in prairie plant communities and under forest canopies as well. In those cases an arbitrary choice placed the species in either the prairie or forest plant group according to the author's experience in obtaining the photograph.

The flora of the western prairies has changed dramatically since Lewis and Clark first explored this region. Much of the open prairie and valleys have been converted to crop land. Virtually all of the land that has not been put to the plow has been grazed and sometimes overgrazed by livestock. Consequently, many species that were once abundant on our prairies have become rare, endangered or even extinct. For that reason, wildflowers should be enjoyed in their natural setting and left for future generations to enjoy. Many species have been introduced either unintentionally or for agriculture and flower gardens.

Some species of wildflowers manage to survive on road edges and unused or waste places. Surprisingly, a few species grow on even the most barren and desolate sites.

In semiarid parts of the West, south facing slopes are typically treeless and therefore have prairie vegetation. North slopes, being more protected from the direct rays of the sun are commonly timbered. One therefore finds prairies and forests intermixed as the aspect of the land changes. It is also common to find prairie plant communities within rather dense forests. Perhaps a rock outcropping or a ridge line occurs in a forest and the soil is too shallow to support trees, thus creating a small forest opening. In many such open spaces in the forest or where trees are scattered, prairie plants thrive.

High elevation prairies sometimes merge directly into subalpine or alpine type vegetation in many parts of the West. Here again an arbitrary choice was necessary, whether to call a particular flower a prairie or an alpine species. As a general rule alpine type vegetation begins between 6,000 and 7,000 feet elevation in the northern part of our region as in Glacier Park, but around 10,000 feet or even higher to the south.

Plants that grow on dry open sites must adapt to high temperatures and a lack of moisture during prolonged periods of time. Some plants, both annual and perennial, have evolved life

6

cycles in which they grow and produce flowers and seeds during the few short weeks of spring when some moisture is available. Others, called biennials, sprout and begin to grow after the first rain in the fall and bloom in the spring.

Still others have developed various structures or methods to store water or conserve moisture in dry climates. Fleshy or succulent stems and leaves serve to store water for plants to use after soil moisture has dissipated. The cacti are best known for this characteristic.

Some plants can close the pores, called stomata, in their leaves to retard water loss during the day when temperatures are high. Others bloom at night and close their flowers or roll up their leaves during the heat of the day.

A coating of wax on plant surfaces provides still another defense mechanism against rapid water loss. Perhaps the most common defense, though, is the growth of hairs on leaves and stems. Hairs shade leaf surfaces and slow or virtually stop the flow of drying wind over those surfaces.

Naming of Plants

Botanists world wide have developed a system of nomenclature that will accomodate any plant. Within this system each flowering, seed-producing plant belongs to a family, genus and species. Families are groups with broad similarities. Each family contains several or many genera (plural of genus) and within each genus there are many unique species. Further classification may also differentiate varieties within a species.

Scientific names have Latin endings and are therefore italicized in print. The family name is usually dropped, because the genus-species binomial sufficiently defines a specific plant. For example, the name *Iris missouriensis* gives the genus first and then the species. The scientific binomial carries an appendage giving the name of the authority(ies) the author recognizes as having originated the proper name.

Most wildflowers also have one or more common names that have come about through general usage. In the interest of space, not all of the common names are given for flowers that have many such names.

Western North America where Prairie Wildflowers in this book occur

Study area where most of the flowers were photographed

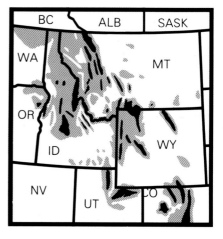

- [ ] Prairies
- Major Forests
- Alpine Zones

Iris Family *(Iridaceae)*

WILD IRIS, Western Blue Flag, Fleur-de-lis

Iris missouriensis Nutt. Large handsome pale to dark blue flowers, often striped with darker blue. Composed of 3 sepals, which are narrow, and 3 broad, drooping or reflexed petals, which have pretty, bright yellow center stripes and throats. A native perennial spreading widely from underground rootstocks. The plants stand 1 to 2 feet tall and have 2 or more smooth narrow leaves sprouting from the base nearly as tall or taller than the flowers. They have 2 to 4 blossoms per stem. Look for Wild Iris in late spring or early summer. HABITAT: Open plains and meadows from low elevation to high in the mountains, sometimes even in open conifer forest, but always where the soil is quite deep and moist or marshy in the spring. RANGE: B.C. to the Dakotas and south to northern Mexico. COMMENT: The only native *Iris* in our region.

GRASS WIDOW

Sisyrinchium inflatum (Suksd.) St. John. Grass Widows have six delicate, open faced 'petals,' reddish or pale bluish purple or occasionally albino, about one inch in diameter. The plants may have one to four blossoms each on smooth stems 6 to 10 inches high. A few grass-like leaves sheath the stem and an upper leaf or bract subtends the flowers and sometimes projects above the flowers. Grass Widow blooms early in the spring soon after snow melt. HABITAT: Prairies at low elevation to open pine forest at medium elevation. RANGE: Idaho to S B.C. east of the Cascades and south to Utah and California. COMMENT: Blue Eyed Grass, *(Sisyrinchium angustifolium),* which has a smaller flower and is deep blue in color, also grows in our region.

Iris Family *(Iridaceae)*

Lily Family *(Liliaceae)*

DOUGLAS' BRODIAEA, Bluedicks

Brodiaea douglasii Wats. Delicate pale blue onion- like flowers, each about 3/4 inch long with dark blue veins in the petals. Six or more flowers per umbel sit atop tall, slender, leafless stems. One or two grassy leaves, somewhat shorter than the flowers, remain bright green at flowering time in April to June.

HABITAT: Prefers grassy prairies or sagebrush plains to open pine forest in the foothills. RANGE: East of the Cascades from B.C. to W Montana and south to N Utah. COMMENT: Seven species of *Brodiaea* inhabit the Pacific Northwest, but only this one grows in the Rockies.

Lily Family *(Liliaceae)*

TEXTILE ONION

Allium textile Nels. & Macbr. The common wild onion of the Great Plains. Dainty white or pinkish flowers with pink or red center stripes on the petals, 15 or more per umbel. Stems round, upright, 3 to 10 inches tall, with two narrow grass-like leaves often taller than the flowers. The single or multiple onion bulb is edible and coated with a persistent, fibrous or textile-like coating. Blooms in the spring. HABITAT: Dry prairies and foothills. RANGE: The Great Plains and west to N Utah, S Idaho and Montana. COMMENT: We have about 70 species of onion native to North America and nearly 30 species in the Pacific Northwest. Onions, garlic, leek and chives are common garden vegetables in this genus, but they have all been introduced from the Old World.

Lily Family *(Liliaceae)*

TAPERTIP ONION *Allium acuminatum* Hook. Exquisite pink to rose-red flowers, 4 to 12 inches high. The petal tips have sharp points and spread widely or curl backward. Leaves are grasslike, shorter than the flowers and usually wither by flowering time in May and June. The small spherical bulb is covered with a thick brown netted coat. HABITAT: Dry hills and open prairie, frequently with bunch-grass. RANGE: Washington, east of the Cascades, to W Montana and south to Arizona. COMMENT: The lilies typically have flower parts in 3's and 6's. If a lily (or an iris) appears to have six petals, it will technically have three sepals and three petals instead.

Lily Family *(Liliaceae)*

GUNNISON'S MARIPOSA, Sego Lily
Calochortus gunnisonii Wats. Large white blossoms, often with two or three flowers on branch ends, they seldom all bloom at once. The flowers are 2 inches or more across. The petals, nearly as broad as long, alternate with three narrow sepals, which are shorter and sharply pointed. The inner faces of the petals have dense hairs near the base over a purple moon- shaped gland. They may have an overall greenish tinge. Blooms in midsummer. HABITAT: Grassy prairies, usually at medium elevation, to open forests. RANGE: Montana to the Black Hills of South Dakota and south to Arizona. COMMENT: Eight species of Mariposa Lily inhabit the Northern Rocky Mountain States.

Lily Family *(Liliaceae)*

SEGO LILY

Calochortus nuttallii Torr. Gorgeous creamy white to lavender blossoms have three large cupped petals with broad shoulders and a stubby pointed tip and three short narrow sepals. The flowers are frequently solitary on un-branched stems, 6 to 20 inches high, but may have more than one blossom. The base of each petal has a round yellow gland surrounded by bright yellow hairs below and a pretty purple crescent above. The flowers overtop several grass-like basal leaves. A few short bract-like leaves may grow on the stem. Sego Lily blooms in late spring and early summer. HABITAT: Sagebrush plains and foothills. RANGE: The Great Plains from North Dakota to New Mexico and west to E Idaho and Nevada. COMMENT: Sego Lily became the State Flower of Utah because early Mormon settlers ate the bulbs in large quantity when they arrived in the vicinity of Great Salt Lake. They considered them 'like manna from heaven.'

Lily Family *(Liliaceae)*

Lily Family *(Liliaceae)*

CAMAS, Blue Camass, Wild Hyacinth

Camassia quamash (Pursh) Greene. Dainty, pale blue to purple (occasionally albino) flowers on a smooth, slender, 8 to 24 inch, unbranched stem. The flowers have short individual flower stalks (a raceme) blooming a few at a time from the bottom upward. Six yellow or blue stamens project outward from six narrow spreading 'petals.' Three or four narrow grass-like leaves grow below the flowers. Blossoms appear in the spring. HABITAT: Loves moist meadows, but also grassy sagebrush flats and even fairly heavily timbered hillsides with deep soil. RANGE: Alberta to Wyoming and west to B.C. and California. COMMENTS: Camas bulbs were a vegetable staple of Indians in the Pacific Northwest before the arrival of white men. Some camas meadows in Idaho appeared to William Clark of Lewis and Clark fame to "resemble a lake of fine clear water, so complete in this deception that on first sight I could have sworn it was water."

CHECKER LILY, Chocolate Lily

Fritillaria atropurpurea Nutt. One to four small, nodding, bell-shaped flowers per stem, mottled purple, brown, yellow and greenish with six prominently protruding stamens. The leaves linear or threadlike, several to many, attached mainly on the upper portion of the stem. One may easily overlook Checker Lily in tall grass. Look for it to bloom in May and June. HABITAT: Open prairie to subalpine ridges and forest clearings. RANGE: The Dakotas to New Mexico and west to the Sierras. COMMENT: Checker Lily has two close relatives, namely Indian Rice *(F. camschatcensis)* and Riceroot *(F. lanceolata),* which both occur along the West Coast.

YELLOW BELL, Yellow Fritillary

Fritillaria pudica (Pursh) Spreng. Pretty yellow harbingers of spring, 4 to 10 inches tall, pendent, bell-shaped perennials. Solitary to three flowers per stem, rising from a scaly bulb. Leaves usually two, oblong and smooth. Flowers may turn orange to dull red with age. Blooms early, March to June depending on elevation. HABITAT: Grassy prairies to sagebrush deserts where moist in the early spring, to open forests and subalpine ridges. RANGE: Northern Rocky Mountain States, west to the foothills of the Cascades. COMMENT: "Consider the lilies of the field, how they grow, they neither toil nor spin; yet I tell you, even Solomon in all his glory was not arrayed like one of these." (Matthew 6:28).

Lily Family *(Liliaceae)*

Lily Family *(Liliaceae)*

STAR LILY, Sand Lily

Leucocrinum montanum Nutt. Striking white, star-shaped flowers nestle in a clump of leaves, barely above ground level. The numerous linear leaves project well above the flowers. Blooms early in the spring. HABITAT: Grassy or sagebrush prairies, usually where sandy or gravelly, to open, well-drained coniferous forest. RANGE: South Dakota to New Mexico and west to E Oregon and the Sierras. COMMENT: Star Lily occurs commonly on the prairies and should not be confused with any other wildflower.

Lily Family *(Liliaceae)*

YUCCA, Spanish Bayonet

Yucca glauca Nutt. Many large, creamy white flowers, 2 to 3 inches across, cover an upright, spike-like stem, 1 to 3 feet high. The flowers tower over a clump of coarse, bayonet-tipped leaves, 8 to 20 inches long. The leaf margins shred raggedly. Flowers appear in June and July. HABITAT: Dry plains to open foothills. RANGE: Southern Alberta to Arizona and east to Iowa and Missouri. COMMENT: Botanists have identified 30 species of *Yucca* in the dry regions of Western America, but just this one can be found in our area.

Lily Family *(Liliaceae)*

MEADOW DEATH CAMAS

Zigadenus venenosus Wats. Unbranched perennial 6 to 20 inches tall, topped by a dense cluster of small white to cream-colored flowers with yellow centers. The leaves are grass-like, several growing from the base and a few much smaller ones on the stem. Blooms in the spring or early summer. HABITAT: Meadows, plains and grassy foothills to alpine ridges. RANGE: Saskatchewan to Nebraska and west to the Pacific Coast, B.C. to Baja. COMMENT: Three species of Death Camas as well as two varieties of *venenosus* grow in our region. All parts of Death Camas are poisonous to humans and livestock. Since it often grows in the same locale as Blue Camas, page 14, and the bulbs of the two look alike, Indians in the early days were careful to harvest camas bulbs when the plants were in bloom or to dig in well-established beds where Death Camas did not occur. Occasional losses of livestock have been attributed to Death Camas.

Milkweed Family *(Asclepiadaceae)*

SHOWY MILKWEED

Asclepias speciosa Torr. Fascinating two-tiered flowers arrayed in a dense umbel. A five-pointed star of horn-like stamens comprises the upper tier, while the lower tier consists of the petals, which bend backward or downward. Pretty bluish pink. The plants, 2 to 3 feet high, spread from an underground root system and have milky sap. Blooms in the summer. HABITAT: Road edges and moist areas at the lower elevations. RANGE: Western and central U.S. and southern Canada, east of the Cascades. COMMENT: May be poisonous to livestock.

Borage Family *(Boraginaceae)*

MINER'S CANDLE, White
Forget-me-not

Cryptantha virgata (Porter) Payson. The most spectacular White Forget-me-not, standing 6 to 40 inches tall. Small round open-faced flowers decorate the tall spikes nearly from top to bottom. Leafy, linear bracts subtend the flowers, projecting outward much beyond the flowers. Leaves, bracts and stems all have coarse, scratchy hairs. Miner's candle blooms in May and June.

HABITAT: Gravelly or grassy slopes and mesas. RANGE: The Rocky Mountain Front, Wyoming and Colorado. COMMENT: Approximately 20 species of white Forget-me-not and one yellow species occur in the Northern Rocky Mountain States, mostly on dry sites. Although this species is distinctive, positive species identification in most cases comes only from technical features of the seeds.

Borage Family (Boraginaceae)

NARROWLEAF BLUEBELL

Mertensia lanceolata (Pursh) DC. An unexpected beauty on the open plains. Narrowleaf Bluebell has one to several stems, 6 to 12 inches high, ending in dense clusters of bright bell- shaped flowers. *Mertensia's* blossoms characteristically have a double bell, first the tube and then the limb or outer bell. The tube and the bell in this species are about the same length. The leaves are narrow and pointed. Look for bluebell flowers in May and June. HABITAT: Open slopes and plains. RANGE: Prairies and valleys on the east side of the Rockies from Alberta to Colorado. COMMENT: Two other species of bluebell occur on our prairies. Both have tubes much longer than the bells. Small bluebell, *M. longiflora,* has broad, blunt leaves while leafy bluebell, *M. oblongifolia,* has long pointed leaves.

Borage Family (Boraginaceae)

YELLOW GROMWELL

Lithospermum incisum Lehm. Bright yellow trumpet-shaped flowers about 1 inch long sprout from the axils of the uppermost leaves. The petals are both scalloped and wavy on the edges. The plants stand 4 to 12 inches high. The leaves are narrow, smooth and sessile. Flowers appear in late April and May.

HABITAT: Open prairies and foothills at low to medium elevation. RANGE: The Great Plains from Canada to Mexico and intermontane valleys from Montana to Utah. COMMENTS: One can also find a close relative, Western Gromwell, *L. ruderale,* throughout our region. It is a larger plant that has smaller flowers with smooth petals.

19

Cactus Family *(Cactaceae)*

PLAINS PRICKLY PEAR, Starvation Cactus

Opuntia polyacantha Haw. Our most abundant cactus, Plains Prickly Pear grows in clumps 6 to 12 inches high, has jointed stems with the pads and joints both flattened. The spines are 1 to 2 inches long and slightly barbed. The pads (stems) function as leaves carrying out photosynthesis, since cacti have no leaves or lose them when young to prevent water loss. The pads are also succulent for storage of water and waxy to conserve water. The flowers, pale lemon yellow and waxy, sometimes have a reddish tinge. Blooms in June and early July. HABITAT: Dry ground at low to mid elevations, often with sagebrush. RANGE: Widespread on both sides of the Rockies from B.C. and Alberta to Mexico. COMMENT: Three species of Prickly Pear occur in the Northern Rocky Mountain States. Cactus plants of all kinds have been collected for home and garden, and some species are threatened with extinction. Native wild cacti should be enjoyed in their natural habitat and left undisturbed.

Caper Family *(Capparidaceae)*   **Cactus Family** *(Cactaceae)*

ROCKY MOUNTAIN BEE PLANT, Stinkweed

Cleome serrulata Pursh. A startlingly
pretty upright annual of stark plains and
desert areas. It stands 1 to 2 1/2 feet
tall, often with several branches, topped
by a dense raceme of irregular,
4-petaled, rose-pink to purple flowers.
The stamens protrude, giving the
flowers a bristly appearance, and the
anthers at the tip of the stamens look
like small coiled worms. Except at first
blooming, long narrow seed pods hang
below the flowers on long slender
pedicels. Look for Rocky Mountain Bee
Plant to bloom from mid to late
summer. HABITAT: Open plains and
foothills, often on roadsides or other
disturbed places. RANGE: The Great
Plains west to the Cascades and
Sierras. COMMENT: Another species,
Yellow Bee Plant, also occurs in our
area, as well as the closely related
Clammy Weed, which has yellowish-
white petals, notched at the tip.

PINCUSHION CACTUS, Nipple Cactus

Coryphanta missouriensis (Sweet) Britt.
& Rose. A small, round, nearly globe-
shaped, stemless cactus, not over 2
inches high. It often appears partially
embedded in the ground. The blossom
is about 1 inch long with numerous
waxy greenish-yellow petals sometimes
tinged with red. Blooms earlier than
Prickly Pear, usually in May and early
June. HABITAT: Desert and plains,
valleys and foothills. RANGE: Mostly
east of the Continental Divide from
Central Montana to Colorado and east
to Manitoba and Kansas. Also in Custer
County, Idaho. COMMENT: Ball or
Cushion Cactus is a similar species with
bright red to purple flowers. The fruit of
Coryphanta is edible and sweet when
ripe.

EVENING CAMPION, Night Flowering Catchfly

Lychnis alba Miller. A rough weedy perennial, 1 1/2 to 3 feet tall, branching freely with pretty white flowers that open at night and close well before noon. The calyx (outermost flower part) forms an inflated tube. The five petals are notched deeply at the tip. The stem leaves grow in opposite pairs, the lower ones with leaf stems, the upper ones smaller and sessile. Look for Evening Campion early in the morning through the summer. HABITAT: Open areas, roadsides and disturbed places, but also on undisturbed sites giving it the appearance of a native plant. RANGE: A European import that is widely established in Western North America. COMMENT: Several species of campion have been introduced into our area. The campions may be confused with various species of catchfly *(Silene),* many of which are also introduced and weedy.

Pink Family *(Caryophyllaceae)*

Pink Family *(Caryophyllaceae)*

MOUSE-EAR CHICKWEED, Field Mouse-ear

Cerastium arvense L. A cheery little perennial that blooms in spring and early summer. It varies from a single stem to densely tufted plants that stand 4 to 20 inches tall. The flowers are about 1/2 inch across and have five petals, deeply notched at the tips.

Leaves, mostly slender and simple, grow in a basal tuft and on the stems. HABITAT: Meadows to dry slopes from valleys to subalpine. RANGE: Temperate northern hemisphere, including most of the U.S. and Canada. COMMENT: This native plant intergrades into Alpine Chickweed, *C. beeringianum,* at high elevations.

22

Axil

Spiderwort Family *(Commelinaceae)*

WESTERN SPIDERWORT
Tradescantia occidentalis (Britt.) Smyth.
Long smooth spidery leaves curve
gracefully outward and down, 6 to 16
inches long, sheathed around the stem
at the base, linear and sharply pointed.
The longest leaves are about the same
length as the upright, rather succulent
stem. The flowers are unique, having
three broad petals, navy blue to pink.
They group tightly in the leaf axils. Look
for this lovely wildflower in May and
June. HABITAT: Prefers rocky or gravelly
sites in the plains, foothills and canyons.
RANGE: The Great Plains from North
Dakota and E Montana south to Texas
and Arizona.

SMALL LEAF PUSSYTOES

Antennaria parvifolia Nutt. Dense clusters of composite flower heads cap several to many upright stems on a low, matted plant. The basal leaves form the mat, are 1/2 to 1 inch long and whitish or gray color from a coating of fine hairs. The stems to 3 inches tall bear linear stem leaves. Careful observation shows a lack of strap-shaped ray flowers. Instead numerous papery bracts, which may vary in color from stark white to bright pink, enclose the floral heads. Blooming varies with elevation from May to July. HABITAT: Dry prairies. RANGE: The Great Plains west to E Washington and Nevada. COMMENT: About 16 species of Pussytoes inhabit our region. One can easily confuse them with Pearly Everlasting, *Anaphalis margaritacea,* which commonly grows in the mountains and forest openings.

Sunflower Family *(Compositae)*

Sunflower Family *(Compositae)*

Pinnate Lobes

TANSYLEAF ASTER

Aster tanacetifolia HBK. This pretty annual Aster grows a single, unbranched stem only 2 to 4 inches high on poor sites, but on better locations, well-developed plants may branch profusely and grow one foot tall or more. Each branch end bears a single blossom. The very distinctive leaves have many deep pinnate lobes and are rather rough and hairy. Flowers appear in late spring and summer. HABITAT: Open prairies and foothills. RANGE: Central Montana to Mexico on the Great Plains. COMMENT: More than 30 species of *Aster* grow in our area, most of them in the mountains. One can also confuse *Asters* with about 30 species of daisies, *Erigeron,* page 29.

24

Sunflower Family *(Compositae)*

ARROWLEAF BALSAMROOT

Balsamorhiza sagittata (Pursh) Nutt. The early spring sunflower of the Inland Empire and Northern Rockies. It grows in a clump from a large taproot that has a strong bitter taste of balsam. Large leaves, shaped like arrowheads to 10 inches long and 2 to 6 inches wide at the base, have smooth edges and are silvery gray with woolly hairs. The flower heads, 2 to 4 inches across, are solitary on long stems that overtop the leaves. Blooms in May and early June. HABITAT: Prefers well-drained soil on open slopes and foothills or open pine forest to near alpine. RANGE: Colorado to Black Hills and west to California and B.C., east of the Cascade-Sierra summit. COMMENT: Most widely distributed and common of the Balsamroots.

TIDY TIPS

Blepharipappus scaber Hook. A pretty little annual to 1 foot tall with white, 3-lobed ray flowers. The purple styles in the floral disc contrast nicely with the white rays. Stems are single or branched and flowers solitary at the ends of the stems and branches. The leaves are very slender or linear, from 1/4 to 1 inch long. It blooms in May. HABITAT: Open bunchgrass foothills and prairies, frequently on rocky or gravelly sites. RANGE: The Blue Mountains of E Oregon and Washington and adjacent Idaho, west to N California.

Sunflower Family *(Compositae)*

Ray ———
Disc —
Composite

Sunflower Family *(Compositae)*

HOARY BALSAMROOT

Balsamorhiza incana Nutt. These flowers are smaller than Arrowleaf Balsamroot and the species has deeply toothed leaves. The stems and leaves carry a dense coat of hairs and are therefore gray in color. Blooms in May and June. HABITAT: Open meadows and slopes to subalpine. RANGE: Southeastern Montana to Wyoming and west to the Blue Mountains of Oregon and Washington. COMMENT: Two other species of Balsamroot with toothed leaves occur in our area. Hairy Balsamroot grows in NE Oregon and Hooker's Balsamroot from S Idaho to Colorado.

26

Sunflower Family *(Compositae)*

Sunflower Family *(Compositae)*

DUSTY MAIDEN, Hoary Chaenactis
Chaenactis douglasii (Hook.) H & A.
These composite flower heads lack ray
flowers, having only white to pink
tubular disc flowers, which are quite
pretty on close examination. Generally a
weedy, unimpressive plant, it often
blends into the background due to its
hairy, dusty appearnce. It stands 12 to
20 inches tall. The leaves, which grow
in a basal rosette as well as on the
stems, are deeply divided up to three
times (fern-like) and do not lie flat.
Blooming may occur from late spring to
the end of summer. HABITAT: Dry often
gravelly locations on prairies and
foothills. RANGE: It grows throughout
our area. COMMENT: Hoary Chaenactis
has four varieties, three of which tend
to hybridize. An alpine species stands
about 3 inches high.

COMMON RABBITBRUSH
Chrysothamnus nauseosus (Pall.) Britt.
Bushy shrubs from 1 to 6 feet high,
they brighten drab plains and deserts in
late summer and fall, sometimes
turning them golden. They are quite
variable in habit. The base is woody but
the twigs are flexible. Leaves are linear
and alternate on the stems. The bright
yellow flowers have 5 to 20 blossoms
per head. Only disc florets are present,
i.e. there are no strap-shaped ray
flowers. HABITAT: Generally dry, open
plains, slopes and foothills, often intermixed with sagebrush on poor,
overgrazed or alkaline soil. RANGE:
From Canada into Mexico, east of the
Cascade-Sierras, to the Great Plains.
COMMENT: Common Rabbitbrush has
six varieties. Two other species of
rabbitbrush occur in the Rockies, but
they prefer mountain habitats.

WAVYLEAF THISTLE

Cirsium undulatum (Nutt.) Spreng.
Coarse native perennial, 1 to 3 feet tall,
often with multiple stems branching
near the top. Leaves on the stems are 2
to 8 inches long, sharply lobed about
halfway to the midrib, the tips of the
lobes armed with short spines. A dense
covering of fine woolly hairs color the
leaves gray or nearly white. The pink to
lavender or purple flower heads are 1
to 1 1/2 inches across. Blooms through
the summer and responds especially
well after a summer shower. HABITAT:
Open prairies and foothills, preferring
well-drained or rocky soil. RANGE: Great
Plains west to central Oregon and
Washington. COMMENT: About 15
species of *Cirsium* grow in our area. At
least two come from Europe as pests.
Most thistle stems and roots are edible
in an emergency.

Sunflower Family *(Compositae)*

Sunflower Family *(Compositae)*

GREAT BASIN RAYLESS DAISY

Erigeron aphanactis (Gray) Greene.
Cheerful little composite flowers in a
low clump, lacking ray florets. They give
the impression of not being fully
opened or mature or being incomplete
without rays. Leaves are basal, growing
from a woody taproot crown,
spatula-shaped and about 3 inches long.
Blooms from May to July. HABITAT:
Prefers dry desert-like locations, often
rocky or gravelly. RANGE: Occasional on
open ridge tops in the Blue Mountains
of NE Oregon to Colorado, Arizona and
California.

Sunflower Family *(Compositae)*

LOW DAISY

Erigeron pumilus Nutt. A clump of small white, pink or blue daisies, composed of 50 to 100 narrow ray flowers and yellow discs. Narrow leaves rise mostly from a woody root crown, but some varieties have a few short linear stem leaves. Blooms in May and June. HABITAT: Prairies and open foothills, frequently with sagebrush. RANGE: Southern B.C. to Saskatchewan and south to New Mexico and S California.

Sunflower Family *(Compositae)*

GAILLARDIA, Blanket Flower

Gaillardia aristata Pursh. Large stately flowers, the central disc purple or brown, the rays deep yellow to almost orange and 3-lobed on the ends. The alternate leaves are usually hairy, 2 to 6 inches long and 1 inch wide. Look for *Gaillardia* in mid to late summer. HABITAT: Meadows and grassy plains to high in the mountains. RANGE: Southern Canada on both sides of the Rockies, south to Colorado and Utah. COMMENT: Very common in late summer throughout our area. A dozen native species of *Gaillardia* grow in Western North America but only one in the Northern Rocky Mountain States.

Sunflower Family *(Compositae)*   **Sunflower Family** *(Compositae)*

THRIFT GOLDENWEED

Haplopappus armerioides (Nutt.) Gray. A low matted perennial with short woody branches that lie prostrate on the ground from which rise a mass of leaves and flower stems. The green leaves are simple, 1 to 3 inches long to 1/4 inch wide. The pretty yellow flowers have 8 to 13 ray florets, which have two or three prominent veins and slight scallops at the tips. Blooms in May and June. HABITAT: Typically very dry rocky slopes and ridges at lower elevations. RANGE: East of the Continental Divide from Montana to Arizona and east to Nebraska. COMMENT: Thrift Goldenweed has a look-alike in Cushion Goldenweed, *H. acaulis.* One finds broad, rounded bracts surrounding the base of the flower heads on Thrift Goldenweed, but sharp pointed bracts on Cushion Goldenweed.

PRAIRIE SUNFLOWER

Helianthus petiolaris Nutt. A small annual sunflower with stems generally 1 to 2 feet tall that may or may not branch. The flowers usually do not exceed 3 inches in diameter and the central disc one inch. This species has simple, lance-shaped leaves. Blooms in the summer. HABITAT: Open plains. RANGE: Southern Alberta to Colorado and east across the plains. COMMENT: A close relative, Common Sunflower, *H. annuus,* grows much larger and may hybridize with Prairie Sunflower. In ancient times, Indians grew them for their valuable seeds. Common Sunflower, the State Flower of Kansas, is the precursor of the cultivated sunflower. Improved varieties now grow around the world.

Sunflower Family *(Compositae)*

STEMLESS HYMENOXYS, Butte Marigold

Hymenoxys acaulis (Pursh) Parker.
Hymenoxys torreyana (Nutt.) Parker.
Stemless Hymenoxys varies considerably over its range with seven varieties generally recognized. The flowers have yellow ray florets, 3-lobed at the tip, and yellow to orange discs (centers). The leaves are simple and usually narrow or linear, growing directly from a woody root crown. Some authors would probably class the dwarf specimen pictured here as a separate species, *H. torreyana*. Blooms from May to July. HABITAT: Open plains from low elevation to near subalpine. RANGE: The Rocky Mountain region and Great Plains.

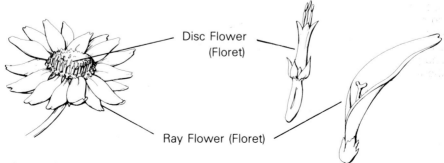

Disc Flower (Floret)

Ray Flower (Floret)

Composite

Sunflower Family *(Compositae)*

Sunflower Family *(Compositae)*

DOTTED GAYFEATHER

Liatris punctata Hook. This showy,
feathery spike of rose-pink to lavender
or purple flowers attracts immediate
attention on otherwise drab prairies.
The flower stems rise in a cluster from
a branching root crown and have
numerous 2 to 4 inch linear leaves. Ray
florets are lacking, but the four to six
disc corollas per flower head are long
and deeply lobed, giving the flower its
feathery appearance. Dotted Gayfeather
blooms in July and August. HABITAT:
Dry plains and foothills. RANGE:
Southern Alberta to Mexico, eastward
on the Great Plains. COMMENT: North
America has about 30 species of *Liatris*,
mostly native and east of our region. It
has one close relative in our area. They
do not look like typical composites,
because the flower heads are elongated
and the disc florets more conspicuous
and pretty than one commonly finds in
the family.   ·

PRAIRIE CONEFLOWER

Ratibida columnifera (Nutt.) W.& S. An
eye-catching, 'different' type of flower,
which consists of a central thimble-
shaped column, 1/2 to 1 1/2 inches
long, covered with a mass of small dark
tubular disc florets. Three to seven
bright yellow ray florets droop below
the thimble. The typical specimen may
branch several times and stand 1 to 4
feet tall. The stem leaves are deeply
lobed, the leaflets narrowly lance-
shaped and sharply pointed at the ends.
Flowers appear in mid summer.
HABITAT: A prairie flower. RANGE:
Alberta to Mexico, east across the Great
Plains. Modern transportation has
extended the range westward along
roads and railroads. COMMENT: In the
southern part of its range, Prairie
Coneflower hybridizes with a close
relative, *R. tagetes,* a smaller prairie
coneflower with deep red rays,
producing occasional specimens with
purple rays.

EARLY TOWNSENDIA, Stemless Daisy
Townsendia hookeri Beaman. One may easily overlook this low tufted plant in dry grass. The white ray flowers ordinarily have a pinkish tinge and contrast with the yellow disc. When fully open, the flower heads are about one inch across. The flowers, virtually stemless, nestle in a low, sparse clump of linear, somewhat succulent leaves. It blooms early, usually in late March and April. HABITAT: Open plains and lower foothills on dry, often sandy or gravelly sites. RANGE: East of the Continental Divide from S Canada to New Mexico. COMMENT: Townsendias typically have large flowers in relation to the rest of the plant and grow singly on individual stems. Nine species of *Townsendia* inhabit the Northern Rockies, four of them quite similar to this one. *T. excapa* appears nearly identical to *hookeri,* but is slightly larger and less common.

Sunflower Family *(Compositae)*

Stonecrop Family *(Crassulaceae)*

LANCELEAVED SEDUM, Yellow Stonecrop *Sedum lanceolatum* Torr. Bright yellow star-shaped flowers, sometimes reddish tinged, crowd the ends of low stems. Some plants have basal leaves and some do not. The leaf is generally 1/2 inch long and fleshy succulent. Some of the leaves usually drop off before the flowers open fully. The stem and leaves may be green, yellow or red. Blooms in late spring and summer. HABITAT: Open rocky outcrops or gravelly sites from sea level to alpine. RANGE: Western North America, north of Mexico. COMMENT: Sedum loves warm roots from the sun shining on its rocky home. Being succulent, it can live through short dry periods or go dormant in times of drouth.

33

Mustard Family *(Cruciferae)*

Mustard Family *(Cruciferae)*

PRAIRIE WALLFLOWER, Prairie Rocket

Erysimum asperum (Nutt.) DC. A tightly packed raceme of pale yellow or occasionally orange flowers top a single or few branched stem, 5 to 20 inches tall. Biennial or perennial with narrow leaves, 1 to 2 inches long. Blooms in spring and early summer. HABITAT: Dry prairies and plains. RANGE: Colorado to Alaska and west to the Cascades. COMMENT: Flowers of the mustard family, *Cruciferae,* typically have four petals in the shape of a cross. It is a very large, complex family with many weedy or inconspicuous species. They tend to inhabit dry ground and many species have been introduced.

GOLDEN DRABA

Draba aurea Vahl. Attractive clumps of bright yellow flowers stand 4 to 12 inches tall, the blossoms 1/4 to 1/2 inch in diameter. Lance-shaped leaves, 1 to 2 inches long, crowd the base of the stem, but grow more open upward. The stems and leaves are quite hairy. The hairs spread in star-burst clusters that require magnification for full appreciation. Golden Draba blooms from April to July depending on elevation. HABITAT: Open foothills to alpine often near scattered ponderosa pine. RANGE: Both sides of the Rockies from Alaska south. COMMENT: We have about two dozen species of *Draba* in the Northern Rockies, most of them yellow or white. Positive species identification is difficult or impossible without the seeds, and one may easily confuse the Drabas with several other genera in the Mustard Family.

Mustard Family *(Cruciferae)*

DESERT PLUME, Prince's Plume

Stanleya pinnata (Pursh) Britt. Stately, unmistakeable, spike-like flowers in racemes. The plants branch from a woody base and stand 1 to 4 feet tall. They bloom from the bottom upward, the feathery flowers composed of four linear petals and six protruding stamens. The basal leaves have pinnate lobes, while the stem leaves grow smaller and simple upward. Flowers appear from late spring into summer. HABITAT: Prairie and desert areas into the foothills. RANGE: The Great Plains from the Dakotas to Texas and west across the Great Basin. COMMENT: Six species of *Stanleya* inhabit the dry areas of the West.

Hydrangea Family *(Hydrangeaceae)*

SYRINGA, Mock Orange

Philadelphous lewisii Pursh. The State Flower of Idaho! Syringa, a shrub to 9 feet high, has showy white 4-petaled flowers that cluster on side branches. They have a very sweet fragrance 'like orange blossoms.' The leaves are generally elliptical or lance-shaped and 1 to 3 inches long. Indians used the straight young shoots for making arrows. Blooms from May to July. HABITAT: Dry rocky hillsides or talus slopes or along stream beds. West of our region Syringa grows in more forested habitats. RANGE: West of the Continental Divide in Montana and Idaho to the Pacific Coast from B.C. to California.

Waterleaf Family *(Hydrophyllaceae)*

St. Johnswort Family *(Hypericaceae)*

THREADLEAF PHACELIA

Phacelia linearis (Pursh) Holz. Several delicate, open-faced blossoms, blue-lavender or pinkish and 1/2 to 3/4 inch across, crowd the tip of the stem as well as short lateral branches on robust specimens. Such broad showy flowers do not typify the waterleaf family. An annual, it stands 5 to 18 inches tall. The leaves are narrow or linear as the names imply and simple, or occasionally they have one or two linear lobes. Threadleaf Phacelia blooms in the spring. HABITAT: Grassy fields, prairies and foothills at low to medium elevation. RANGE: Southern Canada on both sides of the Rockies to Utah and Wyoming.

KLAMATHWEED, Goatweed

Hypericum perforatum L. This perennial branches freely, 1 to 2 1/2 feet tall, and spreads from underground roots. The leaves are narrow to linear and whorled, usually with a large bract-like pair about 1 inch long and two or more smaller leaves at each node. The lower branches tend to leafiness and the upper ones carry terminal clusters of bright yellow flowers about 1/2 inch across. One may need magnification to see the many small black spots which dot the entire plant: stems, leaves and petals. Blooming occurs in June and July. HABITAT: Fields and roadsides in the valleys into forest edges. RANGE: A European import, now common throughout much of our area. COMMENT: Klamathweed is a noxious pest in many localities. It invades pasture and dry range land and may poison livestock, especially sheep, on overgrazed range.

WILD BERGAMOT, Horse Mint

Monarda fistulosa L. Wild Bergamot presents a handsome cluster of rosy pink to blue-lavender, tubular flowers, 1 to 1 1/2 inches long. A whorl of leafy bracts subtends the flower head. All leaves grow on the flower stems, which rise from a spreading root system. The leaves are opposite, lance-shaped and sharply notched or toothed on the edges. The stems have square cross-sections, typical of the Mint Family. Blooms in the summer. HABITAT: Fairly deep moist soil in the valleys and slopes at low to moderate elevation. RANGE: Alberta to Mexico through the Rockies and east across the continent. COMMENT: Could be confused with False Horsemint, *Monardella odoratissimum,* which grows smaller, in clumps and generally west of Wild Bergamot.

Mint Family *(Labiatae)*

Pea Family *(Leguminosae)*

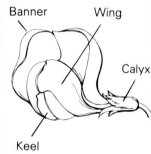

Pea Flower

BARRY'S MATTED PEA

Astragalus Barrii Barneby. This low matted perennial creates a wild jumble of flowers and leaves, spreading along the ground from a woody branching root. Silvery white hairs cover the small 3-lobed leaves. The flowers have blue or purple banner petals and white wing petals. It blooms generally in May.

HABITAT: Open prairies. RANGE: Eastern Montana south to Colorado and probably farther south and east. COMMENT: We have five species of low matted *Astragali* on our plains and prairies. Plains Orophaca, *A. gilviflorus,* is quite common and widespread and has the same general appearance as Barry's Pea, but with white flowers.

Pea Family *(Leguminosae)*

MISSOURI MILKVETCH or Locoweed

Astragalus missouriensis Nutt. Low perennial about 6 inches high with several to many branches growing from a root crown. Three to nine purple flowers cluster at the top of the flower stems. The leaves and stems have a gray cast from many thick straight hairs. The leaves are pinnately compound, the leaflets oval or elliptical and about 1/4 inch long. Blossoms appear in June and July. HABITAT: Open prairies typically with sagebrush. RANGE: The Great Plains, west to the valleys and foothills of the Rockies. COMMENT: *Astragalus* is a very large complex genus. We have about 80 species, many with small, localized ranges.

Pea Family *(Leguminosae)*

WYETH'S LUPINE

Lupinus wyethii Wats. Several to many flower stalks rise in a clump, 1 to 2 feet tall, and well above the leaves. A multitude of flowers on short pedicels crowd the upper third to one half of the stem. The flowers are deep blue to purple and the banner petals are usually lighter; red, yellow or white. Palmately compound leaves with 9 or 11 narrow leaflets grow mostly from the base of the plant. Blooms from May to July. HABITAT: Plains and valleys to subalpine. RANGE: Colorado and California north to S Canada. COMMENT: *Lupinus* is a difficult genus for identification of individual species, because they hybridize extensively.

Pea Family *(Leguminosae)*

RABBITFOOT CRAZYWEED

Oxytropis lagopus Nutt. Low tufted perennial, the stems and leaves densely covered with silky white hairs. The flowers are navy blue or purple, about 1/2 inch long and crowded on the end of a floral stem, forming heads about 1 inch long. The leaves are usually shorter than the flower and pinnate with seven to fifteen oval leaflets, 1/4 to 1/2 inch long. Blooms early—mid April to June. HABITAT: Open plains, often rocky or gravelly places, to scattered timber in the foothills. RANGE: The Great Plains and valleys of Wyoming, Idaho and Montana. COMMENT: Crazyweed may easily be confused with Locoweed *(Astragalus)*. Crazyweed has a pointed beak on the end of the keel petal, while Locoweed does not. We have nine species of *Oxytropis* in the Northern Rockies and three varieties of Rabbitfoot Crazyweed.

Three genera of legumes are poisonous to range livestock when consumed in quantity: Locoweed, Crazyweed and Lupine. Locoweed and Crazyweed are so named because they sometimes give livestock the staggers. Animals will usually bypass these plants, however, unless the range has been overgrazed.

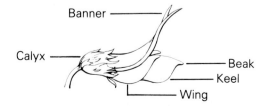

PURPLE PRAIRIE CLOVER

Petalostemon purpureum (Vent.) Rydb. A dense columnar head of small purple flowers and bright yellow stamens, this perennial herb has few to many stems rising 1 to 2 feet tall. The stems frequently branch. The flowers do not resemble the pea-like flowers common to most of our native legumes. They bloom in mid summer, beginning from the base and progressing upward. The flower buds and bases have dense wooly hairs. The leaves are pinnately compound with three to seven short linear leaflets. HABITAT: Open prairie and foothills. RANGE: Northern Great Plains to the foothills of the Rockies, Montana to Colorado. COMMENT: Two other species of prairie clover occur in our area: white prairie clover, *P. candidum,* and western prairie clover, *P. ornatum.*

Pea Family *(Leguminosae)*

Pea Family *(Leguminosae)*

SILKY CRAZYWEED, White Pointloco

Oxytropis sericea Nutt. Silky Crazyweed varies considerably from striking silvery white or even translucent flower heads to pretty cream, pink or yellow ones, sometimes with purple tips on the keel petals. The wing petals spread widely. The leaves, stems and calyx are covered with dense silky hairs. It blooms from late spring to mid summer. HABITAT: Open prairies to alpine ridges. RANGE: The full length of the Rocky Mountain Region, both east and west. COMMENT: Botanists recognize two varieties of Silky Crazyweed: a sheer white to cream or pink variety, somtimes tipped with purple, var. *sericea,* and a yellow one, var. *spicata.*

41

Pea Family *(Leguminosae)*

BIGHEADED CLOVER

Trifolium macrocephalum (Pursh) Poiret. Large elegant solitary flower heads about 2 inches in diameter, pinkish white to rose red, terminate branch ends. The small, low plants may lie prostrate on open uncrowded sites, but stand more or less upright when crowded. The palmately compound leaves have five to seven leaflets— unusual for *Trifolium,* which means three leaved. Look for Bigheaded Clover in the spring. HABITAT: Dry sagebrush plains to high gravelly ridge tops and scattered ponderosa pine forest. RANGE: East slope of the Cascades in Washington to Idaho and south to Nevada. COMMENT: Prettiest of the clovers.

Pea Family *(Leguminosae)*

Pea Family *(Leguminosae)*

PRAIRIE THERMOPSIS, Yellow Pea

Thermopsis rhombifolia Nutt. Patches of bright yellow in the early spring often mark the location of Prairie Yellow Pea. Spreading from underground roots, the stems grow 6 to 16 inches high and usually do not branch. From 10 to 30 flowers closely crowd the stem tips. Three broadly lance-shaped leaflets form a leaf. Blooms in May and June. HABITAT: Prairie and grassland to open woods at medium elevation in the mountains. RANGE: Alberta to Colorado, east to the Dakotas. COMMENT: A taller more robust species, *T. montana,* also grows in our region, usually in wetter more mountainous locales and more westerly than *rhombifolia.*

AMERICAN VETCH

Vicia americana Muhl. ex Willd. Four or more pretty purple or violet 'pea-like' flowers grow in racemes from leaf axils. A perennial herb, 6 to 30 inches tall, stems weak and often reclining. The leaves are pinnately compound and the ends of the leaves elongate to tendrils that may or may not branch and curl. The species varies in the conformation of the leaves and presence or absence of hairs. HABITAT: Open fields and prairies, preferring fairly deep soil. RANGE: Most of North America. COMMENT: A native plant that has several near relatives imported from Europe and Asia.

Blazing Star Family

BLAZING STAR

Mentzelia laevicaulis (Dougl.) T & G.
This coarse, many branched perennial
or biennial, 1 to 3 feet tall bears large
handsome flowers, 2 to 4 inches across.
The lemon yellow flowers have five
lance shaped petals that spread widely
and a multitude of stamens. Blazing
Star opens at night and closes during
the heat of the day. The large leaves
have serrate edges and barbed hairs
that scratch or grab onto clothing. Look
for Blazing Star in mid to late summer.
HABITAT: Dry desert or steep south
facing slopes. RANGE: Montana to
Colorado and central B.C. to California.
COMMENT: Another species of Blazing
Star, *M. decapetala,* has ten petals
instead of five.

44

Flax Family *(Linaceae)*

Four O'Clock Family *(Nyctaginaceae)*

WILD BLUE FLAX, Prairie Flax

Linum perenne var. *lewisii* Pursh.
Several slender stems originate from the top of a woody perennial root. The bright blue, 5-petaled, open faced flowers, 1 to 2 inches in diameter, perch atop the stems. Only a few blossoms open at one time. Leaves are short, linear, upright and closely spaced on the stem. Blooms from May to July. HABITAT: Dry prairie and grassy foothills to subalpine slopes. RANGE: Most of North America west of the Mississippi River as well as Europe and Asia. COMMENT: Our native variety of Wild Blue Flax can only be distinguished from two Old World varieties on technical characteristics. One of the latter was introduced and cultivated extensively for the production of linen fiber and linseed oil. Synthetics have largely replaced flax for these uses.

WHITE SAND VERBENA

Abronia fragrans Nutt. ex Hook.
Hemispherical heads, 2 to 3 inches across, of stark white to cream trumpets make Sand Verbena very distinctive. Papery white bracts subtend the umbellate floral arrangement that has a pleasing fragrance. On well developed plants several stems may spread along the ground from a central taproot. The stem tips and flowers stand upright. The leaves are broadly oval to lance shaped and somewhat succulent. Flowers appear from May to mid summer. HABITAT: Dry sandy areas or on loose dry soil. RANGE: Southern Idaho to the Dakotas, south to Texas and New Mexico. COMMENT: We have three species of Sand Verbena on our prairies.

RED GLOBEMALLOW, Scarlet Falsemallow

Sphaeralcea coccinea (Pursh) Rydb.
Brick red flowers in a terminal cluster, they often grow in patches. The flowers resemble miniature hollyhocks, 1/2 to 3/4 inch in diameter. Palmately compound leaves have irregularly 3-lobed leaflets, speckled with white or yellow star-like clumps of hairs, which give the leaves a rough texture. The flowers emerge from June to early July. HABITAT: Dry grassy prairies and desert areas. RANGE: Very common on the Great Plains from Canada to Mexico and west into Idaho.

Hollyhock (Mallow) Family *(Malvaceae)*

Poppy Family *(Papaveraceae)*

PRICKLY POPPY

Argemone polyanthemos (Fedde) Ownbey. Spectacular flowers, 2 to 3 inches in diameter, have four to six sheer white petals, crumpled from the bud, and many bright yellow stamens. A coarse, branching, thistle-like plant, 2 to 4 feet tall. The leaves are sessile, irregularly toothed and spiny on the margins and the veins. All parts of the plant have yellow prickles except the blossoms. Generally blooms in the summer. HABITAT: Plains and foothills, usually on dry gravelly soil. RANGE: The Great Plains from E Montana and South Dakota to Texas and New Mexico.

Evening Primrose Family *(Onagraceae)*

CLARKIA, Ragged Robin

Clarkia pulchella Pursh. These unique blossoms have four pink or rose and deeply 3-lobed petals, a 4-lobed pearly white stigma and four tightly coiled anthers. Clarkia is an annual herb, 4 to 20 inches long and frequently drooping or supported by grass. It blooms in May and June, sometimes turning entire hillsides bright pink. HABITAT: Loves open grassy hillsides. RANGE: South central B.C. to E Oregon and W Montana. COMMENT: Named for Capt. William Clark of Lewis and Clark fame. The genus, native only to Western America, includes about 30 species. The other species, however, bear little resemblance to this one.

47

Evening Primrose Family *(Onagraceae)*

DESERT EVENING PRIMROSE, Rock Rose

Oenothera caespitosa Nutt. These large elegant flowers have four broad petals shallowly notched at the tip. They grow on a low tufted perennial about 4 to 6 inches high. Both leaves and flowers originate directly from a root crown at or below ground line. The flowers may be numerous, but they open one or two at a time late in the evening or at night and wilt in the heat of the next day. Upon wilting they turn bright pink, usually by mid afternoon, and droop to the ground. Blooms in May and June. HABITAT: Dry flats to arid slopes and road cuts. RANGE: most of Western U.S. and adjacent Canada. COMMENT: Seventeen species of evening primrose inhabit the Northern Rocky Mountain Region.

Evening Primrose Family *(Onagraceae)*

SHRUBBY EVENING PRIMROSE

Oenothera serrulata Nutt. Brilliant yellow, 4-petaled flowers bloom on a low shrub, 6 to 20 inches high. It normally branches profusely. The leaves are narrow, 1 to 2 inches long and finely serrate or toothed on the margins. Look for these refreshing beauties from May to July. HABITAT: Dry prairies, commonly on sandy sites. RANGE: Southeastern Alberta to Arizona, mostly east of the Continental Divide, and eastward. COMMENT: One should not confuse Shrubby Evening Primrose with any other wildflower.

Evening Primrose Family *(Onagraceae)*

HAIRY EVENING PRIMROSE

Oenothera deltoides Torr. & Frem. These flowers appear quite similar to Desert Evening Primrose, but the plants have numerous stems, 2 to 6 inches long, which may stand erect or spread prostrate along the ground. The flowers appear near the ends of the stems but originate in leaf axils. Leaves are of two kinds: simple basal leaves that have smooth or slightly indented margins and deeply toothed stem leaves. HABITAT: Dry plains to sandy desert. RANGE: Eastern Montana to Arizona and California.

49

CLUSTERED BROOMRAPE or CANCERROOT

Orobanche fasciculata Nutt. A small plant, to 6 inches high, with one or more fleshy upright stems. Four to ten flower stalks cluster near the top of the stems. A root parasite, usually attached to the roots of sagebrush, it lacks green leaves and depends on its host plant for sustenance. Notice the leaves of the host, Silver Sage, in the picture. The flowers resemble penstemons, but are not related. Quite pretty on close inspection, the flowers appear in late spring and early summer. HABITAT: Prairies and foothills, always with other plants. RANGE: Most of Western North America, south to northern Mexico. COMMENT: We have five species of *Orobanche*.

Broomrape Family *(Orobanchaceae)*

Evening Primrose Family *Onagraceae)*

SCARLET GAURA

Gaura coccinea (Nutt.) Pursh. A graceful spidery flower, easy to overlook in grassy places. Several weak stems branch freely. They are covered with linear to lance-shaped leaves that grow smaller upward and are tipped with a dense spike of flowers. Only one or a few flowers bloom at one time—June and July. HABITAT: Dry prairies and valleys with grasses or sagebrush. RANGE: Mainly east slope of the Rockies, but also the intermontane valleys of Montana and S Idaho. COMMENT: Unique. Should not be confused with any other wildflower.

50

SCARLET GILIA, Sky Rocket

Gilia aggregata (Pursh) Spreng. Bright red trumpets, 3/4 to 1 1/2 inches long, several to many on an unbranched stem to 2 feet tall. The flowers all tend to grow on one side of the stem. The throats of the flowers, which are often speckled yellow or white, flare into five sharp pointed petals. Leaves are lacy, deeply lobed and grow mostly from the base of the plant. Look for these beauties in June and July. HABITAT: Dry grassy hills and plains, often among scattered conifers, to medium elevation in the mountains. RANGE: Southern Canada to Mexico in the Rockies and Great Basin. COMMENT: In Colorado and southward one finds a cream colored variety, treated as a separate species by some authors. It frequently hybridizes with the scarlet flowers producing various shades of pink.

Phlox Family *(Polemoniaceae)*

Phlox Family *(Polemoniaceae)*

HOOD'S PHLOX

Phlox hoodii Rich. Low perennial forms a dense cushion from a single taproot. Multiple stems spread along the ground and upright branches rise 1 to 4 inches. White or pink flowers, solitary on the branch ends, flare to about 1/2 inch across. The tiny leaves are needle shaped and cover the stems. Hood's Phlox blooms early—April to June. HABITAT: Dry plains and foothills. RANGE: Nebraska and Colorado to the Yukon and west to the Cascades. COMMENT: Perhaps no other genus typifies spring wildflowers on the prairies and foothills better than *Phlox*.

Phlox Family *(Polemoniaceae)*

CUSHION PHLOX

Phlox pulvinata (Wherry) Cronq. A low mat former similar to Hood's Phlox, but with larger flowers and without woody stems. The leaves grow larger, to 1/2 inch long. One can easily confuse this cushion Phlox with *Phlox caespitosa*. Blooms from mid spring to early summer. HABITAT: Gravelly or rocky locations from medium to high elevations. RANGE: Southern Montana to E Oregon and south through the Rocky Mountain Region. COMMENT: Of the 17 species of *Phlox* in our area, most of them occur on the prairies. Phlox of one species or another is nearly ubiquitous on all undisturbed prairie sites.

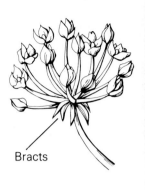

Bracts

Umbel

Buckwheat Family *(Polygonaceae)*

YELLOW ERIOGONUM

Eriogonum flavum Nutt. This yellow buckwheat forms a dense low mat of many crowded, narrowly lance shaped leaves. The flower stems rise 2 to 10 inches high without stem leaves, but a whorl of leafy bracts top the stems and subtend the floral umbels. The leaves, stems and bracts are quite hairy and grayish color. Flowers appear in late spring and early summer. HABITAT: Rocky or gravelly outcrops in the prairies and foothills to alpine ridges. RANGE: Colorado north to S Alberta and B.C. COMMENT: Yellow Eriogonum has a near look-alike in Sulphur Flower, *E. umbellatum.*

Buckwheat Family *(Polygonaceae)*

WYETH BUCKWHEAT

Eriogonum heracleoides Nutt. These flowers form a compound umbel of white or creamy blossoms, turning pink with age. The umbel has a whorl of leafy bracts underneath. A perennial that spreads from a woody base with many narrow or lance shaped leaves. The unbranched flower stems, 4 to 12 inches high, have a whorl of leaves about mid height. Blooms from May to July. HABITAT: Gravelly plains and foothills. RANGE: B.C. to Montana, south to Wyoming and California. COMMENT: We have over 20 species of *Eriogonum,* chiefly in dry open spaces.

NEVADA PYGMY BITTERROOT

Lewisia pygmaea var. *nevadensis* (Gray) Fosberg. Low perennial rising from a carrot shaped taproot. It is similar to Bitterroot (back cover) in conformation, but the flowers are smaller and have fewer petals that are white, yellowish white or pale pink. The leaves are succulent, to 6 inches long, and stay green throughout the blooming period in June and July. HABITAT: High gravelly plains to subalpine reaches. RANGE: High ridge tops of SE Washington, south and west through the Great Basin to S California. Rare in the Central Rockies. COMMENT: The type variety, *L. pygmaea* var. *pygmaea,* is even smaller than *nevadensis,* has bright pink flowers and ranges throughout most of the alpine regions of Western U.S.

Purslane Family *(Portulacaceae)*

Primrose Family *(Primulaceae)*

ROCKY MOUNTAIN DOUGLASIA

Douglasia montana Gray. A pretty mass of pink to rose colored flowers that brighten drab prairies in spring or early summer. These mat forming plants have rosettes of needle shaped leaves about 1/4 inch long and short flower stalks that rise from the rosettes. Pistils and stamens do not project out of the short floral tubes, which have bright yellow throats. HABITAT: High plains and open foothills to high mountain ridges. RANGE: Southwestern Alberta to Wyoming and Idaho. COMMENT: One could easily mistake this member of the primrose family for a *Phlox,* but the lack of noticeable stamens and pistils helps to identify it.

Buttercup Family *(Ranunculaceae)*

PASQUEFLOWER, Prairie Crocus

Anemone nuttalliana DC. The State Flower of South Dakota! These handsome pale blue to purple flowers remind one of tulips. There may be one or several stems in a cluster, 2 to 10 inches high. They rise from a deep root system. The lacy basal leaves have long petioles, but the leaves on the flower stem grow in a whorl. A dense coating of fine hairs cover the stems and leaves. Pasqueflower blooms early in the spring, sometimes creating extensive natural gardens. HABITAT: Grassy prairies to scattered ponderosa pine forests in the foothills and mountains. RANGE: Most of the Great Plains, west to Central Washington and S Alaska. COMMENT: We have eight species of *Anemone* in our area and they are some of our most attractive wildflowers.

SUGARBOWL, Vaseflower

Clematis hirsutissima Pursh. This is an extraordinary cup-like flower, light to dark blue on the outside and dark blue on the inside. A mass of yellow stamens fills the throat of the cup. They are easy to overlook because the flowers nod or droop. The plant grows in a clump with several stems 1 to 2 feet high and opposite, deeply divided or lacy leaves. Blooms in the spring. HABITAT: Grassy prairie to scattered pine woods. RANGE: Montana and Wyoming to Central Oregon and S B.C. COMMENT: Might be confused with two other species of *Clematis,* but they are vines that normally grow under a forest canopy.

Buttercup Family *(Ranunculaceae)*

Buttercup Family *(Ranunculaceae)*

WESTERN WHITE CLEMATIS, Virginsbower

Clematis ligusticifolia Nutt. Climbing woody vines that form dense covers on fences, shrubs and even trees. Technically the flowers have five or six sepals but no petals and are normally less than one inch across. The leaves are pinnately compound with five to seven leaflets, irregularly toothed. Blooming period is late spring and early summer. HABITAT: Valleys and sagebrush plains to forest margins, where the soil is fairly deep and moist. RANGE: Central B.C. to Alberta and south to California and New Mexico.

56

Buttercup Family *(Ranunculaceae)*

LITTLE LARKSPUR, Montana Larkspur
Delphinium bicolor Nutt. This showy perennial displays several irregular navy-blue flowers on a simple stem, 3 to 15 inches tall. Five stylish, widespreading sepals attract immediate attention. The upper sepal extends backward forming a long conical spur. The four petals are much smaller than the sepals. An upper pair is white with blue lines. A lower pair, dark blue and inconspicuous, blends with the sepals. Leaves are palmately compound and deeply parted into slender leaflets. Blooms in springtime. HABITAT: Grassy prairies to scattered coniferous forest. RANGE: Our Northern Rocky Mountain Region into Saskatchewan. COMMENT: Some authors call low species 'Larkspurs' and tall ones 'Delphinium,' while others consider annuals to be the 'Larkspurs' and perennials 'Delphinium.' In scientific nomenclature they are all *Delphinium*.

PRAIRIE SMOKE, Purple Avens

Geum triflorum Pursh. One to several, but usually three, top-shaped flowers nod gracefully in the prairie breeze. They are brick red or yellowish with red stripes. The outer sepals nearly hide the light-yellow petals. The fruit becomes puffs of long feathery plumes that travel on the wind. The leaves divide into many segments. Blooming occurs early in the spring or into summer at high elevation. HABITAT: Open prairie and foothills where the soil is quite deep and moist in the spring, to meadows above timberline. RANGE: The northern third of continental U.S. east of the Cascades and much of Canada.

Rose Family *(Rosaceae)*

Buttercup Family *(Ranunculaceae)*

SAGEBRUSH BUTTERCUP

Ranunculus glaberrimus Hook. Bright, cheerful yellow blossoms that are often the first wildflowers of spring. Five spreading sepals (no petals) surround a mound of greenish-yellow stamens. The leaves, mostly basal, may be simple entire or 3- lobed. Sagebrush Buttercup blooms soon after snowmelt from March to May. HABITAT: Sagebrush prairies and open hills to scattered ponderosa pine woods. RANGE: Pacific Northwest to the northern Great Plains. COMMENT: The common early spring buttercup in our region.

PRAIRIE CINQUEFOIL

Potentilla pennsylvanica L. A tufted plant with many branches, 10 to 20 inches high, originating on a woody root. The leaves have five to nine pinnate leaflets that are also pinnately lobed about halfway to the midrib. Dense silky hairs cover the underside of the leaflets. The flowers are round and open-faced, typical of *Potentilla,* with five pale yellow petals and a dark yellow center composed of many stamens and pistils. Blooms from May into summer. HABITAT: Prairie grassland and foothills to mountain openings. RANGE: Much of North America from the Arctic nearly to Mexico. COMMENT: About 15 species of Cinquefoil inhabit our plains and prairies.

Rose Family *(Rosaceae)*

Rose Family *(Rosaceae)*

CHOKECHERRY

Prunus virginiana L. A round columnar mass of pleasing white flowers on a shrub or small tree. The leaves are oval or elliptic, 2 to 4 inches long, with small serrate teeth on the edges and pointed at the tip. The fruits are small seedy cherries, dark red to black when ripe, and have a bitter taste that is not altogether unpalatable after the first one! Makes gourmet jam or jelly. Blooms in late spring or early summer. HABITAT: Open valleys and grassy prairies, usually where the soil is deep and well-watered, such as stream banks. RANGE: Temperate North America. COMMENT: We have just one variety in our area.

Rose Family *(Rosaceae)*

WILD PRAIRIE ROSE

Rosa arkansana Porter. Gorgeous bright pink roses, 2 to 3 inches across. The State Flower of North Dakota! The flowers may fade to white with age or white streaked with pink. Wild Prairie Rose typically has stems 3 to 12 inches long, a few flowers clustered on the end of the main stem of the current year. The stems normally die back to or near the ground each year. On protected sites the plant may become a true shrub standing 5 to 6 feet tall. Many short straight prickles cover the stems. Blooms in June and July. HABITAT: Open prairies. RANGE: The Great Plains from central Canada to Texas and the Rockies to Missouri.

Rose Family *(Rosaceae)*

Sandalwood Family *(Santalaceae)*

ANTELOPE BRUSH, Bitterbrush

Purshia tridentata (Pursh) DC. A spreading many- branched shrub, 2 to 10 feet high, with distinctive leaves less than one inch long and 3-lobed on the ends. Branches typically have numerous stubby side shoots which bear solitary flowers. The flowers have five yellow petals and many stamens. After a brief blooming period in the spring, the petals fall off early. HABITAT: Dry hills and plains to the fringes of ponderosa pine forest. RANGE: Western U.S. and southern B.C., east of the Cascades. COMMENT: Named for Frederick Pursh, the botanist who first catalogued the plant specimens collected by Lewis and Clark. Game animals often browse on Antelope Brush.

PALE BASTARD TOADFLAX

Comandra umbellata (L.) Nutt. Clusters of tiny bell- shaped flowers mottled or variably colored red, greenish, yellowish or white on the same plant. The unbranched stems are 3 to 12 inches high and grow in patches from spreading underground roots. The rather fleshy leaves alternate on the stems. Blooms in the spring. HABITAT: Dry plains and prairies on sandy or gravelly soil to subalpine slopes. RANGE: Southwestern Canada and Western U.S.

Saxifrage Family *(Saxifragaceae)*

Saxifrage Family *(Saxifragaceae)*

SLENDER FRINGECUP, Woodland Star

Lithophragma tenella Nutt. These saucy little saucer- shaped flowers have five white or pinkish petals that are deeply 5-lobed. Stems are slender but upright, unbranched and quite hairy. Leaves palmately compound, the leaflets irregularly 3- to 7-lobed. Look for Fringecups early in the spring. HABITAT: Grassy or sagebrush prairies and hills to scattered coniferous forest. RANGE: Alberta to Colorado, Arizona and westward. COMMENT: We have four species of Fringecup identifiable on technical characters.

WESTERN SAXIFRAGE, Redwool Saxifrage

Saxifraga occidentalis Wats. Pyramidal or flat-topped heads of tiny white or pinkish flowers sit atop reddish woolly stems. Typical of most saxifrages, the stems are leafless and unbranched. The leaves form a rosette at the base of the stem. They have teeth on the edges and frequently reddish color on the underside. Flowers appear early depending on elevation. HABITAT: High prairies or meadows to alpine, where moist in the early spring but drying by mid summer. RANGE: Northwestern U.S. and SW Canada. COMMENT: Most saxifrages love to keep their feet wet on rocky cliffs and stream banks, but this species is an exception. More than 20 species of *Saxifraga* occur in our region. Western Saxifrage also has six varieties, causing considerable variation in appearance of the species.

WYOMING BESSEYA, Wyoming Kittentail

Besseya wyomingensis (Nels.) Rydb. These fascinating little flowers lack petals, but the dense cylindrical flower heads bristle with dark red stamens. A perennial, 3 to 10 inches tall, the leaves are gray-hairy and often reddish tinged, the lance-shaped basal leaves 1/2 to 1 inch long, the stem leaves smaller. Blooms soon after snowmelt. HABITAT: High open prairie and foothills to subalpine. RANGE: Alberta to N Utah, east to South Dakota and W Nebraska. COMMENT: Two other species of Besseya grow in our region: Red Kittentail, *B. rubra,* a larger version which ranges farther west, and *B. alpina,* which inhabits the high mountains in the southern part of our region.

Figwort Family *(Scrophulariaceae)*

Figwort Family *(Scrophulariaceae)*

DOWNY PAINTEDCUP

Castilleja sessiliflora Pursh. Long curved floral tubes or corollas extend gracefully beyond the slender 3-lobed bracts. The inflorescence tinted pink, purple, green or yellow varies in multiple combinations of these colors. Blooms from May to July. HABITAT: Dry prairies. RANGE: The Great Plains from the Mississippi River to the Rocky Mountain Front and S Manitoba to Texas. COMMENT: A common paintbrush of the open plains, it has no near relatives in our area.

63

Figwort Family *(Scrophulariaceae)*

NARROWLEAF INDIAN PAINTBRUSH
Castilleja angustifolia (Nutt.) G. Don. A
stunning little perennial in drab arid hills.
Greenish-purple stems accent the bright
pink to magenta, purplish or
occasionally yellow flowers. The leaves
divide into narrow or linear segments.
Few to several hairy stems rise 3 to 14
inches from a woody root crown.
Blooms in spring or early summer.

HABITAT: Desert, prairie and foothills.
RANGE: Southern Montana and
Wyoming to S Idaho and E Oregon.
COMMENT: *Castilleja* is a very difficult
genus in which to identify individual
specimens, because many species
hybridize quite freely. This species,
though rather limited in range, is fairly
distinct. It is on Montana's rare species
list.

Figwort Family *(Scrophulariaceae)*

Figwort Family *(Scrophulariaceae)*

SLENDER INDIAN PAINTBRUSH

Castilleja gracillima Rydb. An attractive greenish- yellow to red paintbrush that grows in clumps from a deep spreading root system. The flower bracts are simple and rounded or have two small lateral lobes. They vary in height from 4 to 16 inches and bloom in July and August. HABITAT: Grassy meadows from medium elevation to near alpine. RANGE: Idaho, Montana and Wyoming. COMMENT: We have six species of yellow paintbrush, or species that have yellow forms, on our prairies.

DALMATION TOADFLAX

Linaria dalmatica (L.) Mill. Pretty yellow flowers resembling snapdragons with orange beards in the throats. The inflorescence is a spike-like raceme on one to several branches. A bluish glaucus bloom coats the broad leaves, which are sessile and clasp the stem. The plants stand 1 to 3 feet tall and spread from underground roots. Flowers appear in late spring and early summer. HABITAT: Dry gravelly areas, especially roadsides. RANGE: Native to Eurasia, now established in many localities in our region. COMMENT: Butter-and-eggs is a close relative, also introduced, a smaller plant with narrow leaves.

Figwort Family *(Scrophulariaceae)*

WYOMING INDIAN PAINTBRUSH

Castilleja linariaefolia Benth. One of our most beautiful wildflowers, the State Flower of Wyoming! A bushy clump of upright stems, 4 to 24 inches tall, often branching, topped by crimson or occasionally yellowish paintbrushes. The flower bracts and the outer floral sheaths or calyces have the bright coloration. The bracts are 3-lobed, the lobes as well as the stem leaves are narrow or linear as the name implies. Blooms from late spring to mid summer. HABITAT: Open prairie, usually with sagebrush, to fairly high elevation in the mountains. RANGE: Southern Montana to E Oregon and south to New Mexico and Arizona. COMMENT: Wyoming Indian Paintbrush creates crimson splashes amidst the dull green of sagebrush or turns entire hillsides bright red.

Figwort Family *(Scrophulariaceae)*

Figwort Family *(Scrophulariaceae)*

YELLOW OWL CLOVER

Orthocarpus luteus Nutt. This small annual has showy pink bracts that resemble Indian Paintbrushes, but paintbrushes are perennials. The stems, 4 to 12 inches tall, ordinarily do not branch, but exceptions do occur. Bright yellow tubular flowers mostly hide behind the bracts. Leaves are linear and opposite on the flower stems. Look for these beauties in the summer. HABITAT: Open grassy prairies and foothills. RANGE: Minnesota and Nebraska west to the Cascade-Sierras.

FERNLEAF LOUSEWORT

Pedicularis cystopteridifolia Rydb. Beautiful blood- red to reddish-purple floral heads stand 4 to 16 inches tall. The leaves are deeply incised pinnately and fernlike, growing smaller upward. Blooms appear from June to August. HABITAT: Open meadows and grassy slopes from medium elevation to near alpine. RANGE: Wyoming and Montana. COMMENT: This species could be called a mountain or subalpine dweller along with several other species of Lousewort.

Figwort Family *(Scrophulariaceae)*

FUZZYTONGUE PENSTEMON

Penstemon eriantherus Pursh. These large tubular blossoms, 1 to 2 inches long, have broad mouths. An instantly captivating wildflower, the feature that attracts immediate attention is the bright yellow hairiness filling the open throat of the flower tube. The name *Penstemon* means five stamens, and one of them is always sterile. In this species the fuzzy tongue that one notices is the anther at the end of the sterile stamen that is covered with long hairs. The leaves are narrow and toothed on the margins. Blossoms appear from late May to July. HABITAT: Dry prairies and foothills. RANGE: The Columbia Basin to Nebraska. COMMENT: About 30 species of *Penstemon* can be found in the Northern Rockies, the majority of them in the mountains.

Figwort Family *(Scrophulariaceae)*   Figwort Family *(Scrophulariaceae)*

SHINING PENSTEMON

Penstemon nitidus Dougl. Several whorls of bright blue blossoms surround one or several stems, 4 to 12 inches tall. The plant branches from a taproot. The leaves set this attractive species apart. They are broad, quite thick or almost fleshy, smooth and have a gray-blue glaucus coating. The basal leaves grow in a tuft and have fairly long stems. The leaves on the flower stalks are opposite and stemless, clasping the stalks and nearly enclosing them. Look for this pretty wildflower in the spring. HABITAT: Plains, open valleys and foothills, frequently on roadsides and other disturbed ground. RANGE: South-central Canada to Wyoming.

BEAUTIFUL TONELLA

Tonella floribunda Gray. Cheerful showy little annual or biennial with blue and white flowers. The leaves opposite and 3-parted or whorled. Blooms in the spring. HABITAT: Open slopes and bunchgrass foothills and canyons. RANGE: Limited to the Blue Mountains of E Oregon and Washington and adjacent Idaho.

Parsley (Carrot) Family *(Umbelliferae)*

BISCUITROOT, Large Fruited Desert Parsley

Lomatium macrocarpum (Hook. & A.) C & R. Above ground this plant resembles Couse, but has white or slightly purplish flowers instead. One to several flowers on smooth, unbranched stems rise 4 to 10 inches from the top of a long thick taproot. Many small, lacy segments, gray or purplish-green, comprise the leaves. Blooms in the spring. HABITAT: Open prairies. RANGE: Southern B.C. to Manitoba and south to Utah. COMMENT: Indians used to dig the roots for food. They would dry them, pound them into flour and make thin loaves of bread.

Parsley (Carrot) Family *(Umbelliferae)*

COUSE, Cous

Lomatium cous (Wats.) C & R. A species prized for food in the early days by Indians. The root expands into a large edible tuber. A mass of tiny yellow flowers are arranged in compound umbels (twice umbellate). In this species the arms of the umbel are typically unequal in length. Flowers appear in spring. HABITAT: Dry hills and sagebrush prairies. RANGE: Central Oregon and Washington to Montana and Wyoming. COMMENT: We have about 15 species in this large diverse family. While many native species have edible roots, we also have some species that are deadly poisonous!

70

Parsley Family *(Umbelliferae)*

Parsley Family *(Umbelliferae)*

TURKEY PEA, Indian Potato

Orogenia linearifolia Wats. Our earliest wildflower, Turkey Pea blooms in February at low elevation in the Blue Mountains, weather permitting. It grows only 1 to 3 inches tall, a compound umbel, the arms of the umbel unequal in length. The flowers are white with a purplish cast imparted by the stamens. The flower stem and the parted, linear leaves originate from a small spherical tuber. HABITAT: Dry, often rocky meadows in the valleys to the foothills. RANGE: Southeastern Washington to W Montana, south to W Colorado and Utah. COMMENT: Some Indians eagerly sought this delightful little plant as the first available vegetable in the spring. They ate the tubers raw, roasted or boiled. Digging enough for a meal, however, would be a real chore.

YAMPAH, Squaw Root

Perideridia gairdneri (H & A) Mathias. A white compound umbel with dense heads of tiny flowers. A single stem grows from an edible top-shaped root. Leaves are few and grasslike with one or two pinnate forks. The plant, 15 to 20 inches tall or taller, may hide in long meadow grass. Flowers appear in July and August. HABITAT: Prairie and grassy meadows to scattered woods. RANGE: Southern B.C. to Saskatchewan, south to S California and New Mexico. COMMENT: Yampah, an Indian name, was an important food for many western tribes. Sacajawea taught members of the Lewis and Clark expedition how to dig 'wild carrots.'

Violet Family *(Violaceae)*

PRAIRIE VIOLET, Valley Yellow Violet

Viola nuttallii Pursh. Merry little yellow perennial, it grows in a tuft of lance- or nearly heart-shaped leaves. The upper petal sometimes has purple on the back and the lower three petals have purple stripes called guide lines, thought by some to guide pollinating insects to the flowers. Blossoms appear from April to July. HABITAT: Dry prairie to open conifer edges in the foothills to moist woods. RANGE: Western half of temperate North America. COMMENT: This species ranges widely and is quite variable. Some botanists assign five varieties to the one species, while others call them five separate species. We also have three other species of yellow violet as well as several blue ones in the Northern Rocky Mountain States.

Selected references

1. Booth, W.E. and J.C. Wright. *Flora of Montana, Part II.* Montana State U. Bozeman. 1959.

2. Clark, Lewis J. *Wild Flowers of the Pacific Northwest.* Gray's. Sidney, B.C. 1976.

3. Craighead, John J., F.C. Craighead and R.J. Davis. *A Field Guide to Rocky Mountain Wildflowers.* Houghton Mifflin. Cambridge. 1963.

4. Dorn, Robert D. *Vascular Plants of Montana.* Mountain West. Cheyenne. 1984.

5. Harrington, H.D. *Edible Native Plants of the Rocky Mountains.* U. of New Mexico. Albuquerque. 1976.

6. Haskins, Leslie L. *Wild Flowers of the Pacific Coast.* Metropolitan. Portland. 1934.

7. Hitchcock, C. Leo, A. Cronquist, M. Ownbey and J.W. Thompson, eds. *Vascular Plants of the Pacific Northwest,* in 5 Vols. U. of Wash. Seattle. 1955 to 1969.

8. Hitchcock, C. Leo and A. Cronquist. *Flora of the Pacific Northwest.* U. of Wash. Seattle. 1973.

9. Johnson, James R. and J.T. Nichols. *Plants of South Dakota Grasslands.* Bulletin 566. South Dakota State U. Brookings. 1970.

10. Larrison, Earl J., G.W. Patrick, W.H. Baker and J.A. Yaich. *Washington Wildflowers.* Seattle Audubon Soc. 1974.

11. Lesica, P. et. al. *Vascular Plants of Limited Distribution in Montana.* Montana Acad. of Sci. 1984.

12. Lyons, C.P. *Trees Shrubs and Flowers to Know in Washington.* Evergreen. Vancouver. 1956.

13. Moss, E.H. *Flora of Alberta.* U. of Toronto. 1959.

14. Nelson, Burrell E. *Vascular Plants of the Medicine Bow Range.* Jelm Mt. Press. Laramie. 1984.

15. Niehaus, Theodore F. and C.L. Ripper. *A Field Guide to Pacific States Wildflowers.* Houghton Mifflin. Boston. 1976.

16. Orr, Robert T. and M.C. Orr. *Wildflowers of Western America.* Galahad. N.Y. 1981.

17. Shaw, Richard J. and D. On. *Plants of Waterton-Glacier National Parks.* Mountain Press. Missoula. 1979.

18. Spellenberg, Richard. *The Audubon Society Field Guide to North American Wildflowers, Western Region.* Knopf. N.Y. 1979.

19. St. John, Harold. *Flora of Southeastern Washington.* Edwards Bros. 1963.

20. Van Bruggen, Theodore. *Wildflowers of the Northern Plains and Black Hills.* Badlands Nat. Hist. Assoc. Interior, S.D. 1971.

21. Vance, F.R., J.R. Jowsey, and J.S. McLean. *Wildflowers of the Northern Great Plains.* U. of Minn. Minneapolis. 1984.

22. Venning, Frank D. *Wildflowers of North America.* Golden. N.Y. 1984.

23. Weber, William A. *Rocky Mountain Flora.* Colorado U. Boulder. 1976.

Illustrated Glossary

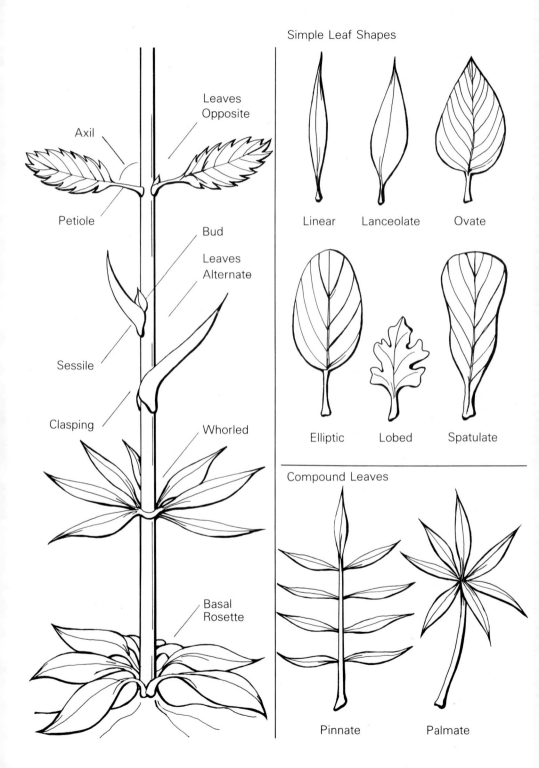

Axil

Petiole

Leaves
Opposite

Bud

Leaves
Alternate

Sessile

Clasping

Whorled

Basal
Rosette

Simple Leaf Shapes

Linear   Lanceolate   Ovate

Elliptic   Lobed   Spatulate

Compound Leaves

Pinnate   Palmate

Glossary

Annual— A plant that completes its life cycle in one year.
Anther— The pollen-producing appendage on the stamen.
Axil— The upper angle formed between a leaf stem and a branch.
Basal— At the base of the plant, the ground line.
Biennial— Living for part or all of two years.
Bract— A leaf-like scale on a flower cluster.
Bulb— A plant bud usually below ground.
Calyx— The outermost portion of a flower, the sepals collectively.
Clasping— As a leaf base surrounding a stem.
Corolla— The petals collectively.
Disc flower or floret— Tubular flowers at the center of a composite head.
Gland— A spot or expanded area that produces a sticky substance.
Glaucus— Fine powder coating a surface.
Head— A cluster of flowers crowding the tip of a stem.
Herb— A plant that dies back to the ground annually.
Hybrid— Pollination of a plant by another species or variety.
Inflorescence— An arrangement of flowers on a stem.
Midrib— The central vein of a leaf.
Node— A point on a stem where leaves or branches originate.
Parted— Separated or lobed.
Pedicel— The supporting stem of a single flower.
Perennial— A plant that lives more than two years.
Petal— The floral leaves inside the sepals.
Petiole— The supporting stem of a leaf.
Pistil— The female organ of a flower.
Raceme— An inflorescence on a common stalk composed of flowers on pedicels.
Ray flowers or florets— Strap-shaped flowers in a composite head.
Sepal— The outermost floral leaves, one segment of the calyx.
Serrate— With short sharp teeth on the margin.
Sessile— Lacking a stem or pedicel, attached at the base.
Sheathed— Enclosing a stem at the base, clasping.
Shrub— A woody plant smaller than a tree.
Spike— An inflorescence of sessile flowers on a common stalk.
Stamen— The pollen-producing organ of a flower.
Stigma— The end of the pistil that receives the pollen.
Style— The slender stalk of a pistil.
Subtend— Located directly beneath a flower or other structure as if supporting it.
Succulent— Pulpy, soft and juicy.
Taproot— A central vertical root.
Tendril— A slender twining extension of a leaf or stem.
Tuber— A thickened underground stem.
Tubular— In the form of a tube.
Tuft— A clump or close group of stems and/or leaves.
Umbel— A group of stems or pedicels that arise from a common point on a stalk.
Whorl— Three or more leaves or branches growing from a node or common point.

Index

Hints on Photographing Wildflowers

Modern cameras make wildflower photography possible for anyone who wishes to enjoy it as a hobby. A reasonably priced single lens reflex camera is the choice of many wildflower enthusiasts. More important than the make of camera is the lens or lenses one uses. Many choices are available and there is no one best lens. A medium length telephoto lens will double for larger wildflowers, scenery and animal shots, but a good closeup lens is essential for small flower specimens.

When taking a wildflower picture, look through the view finder and compose the picture desired. What you see is just about what you get. Pay particular attention to the background. Too much dry grass, dead leaves or old stalks will ruin an otherwise excellent picture. It is often necessary to do some 'gardening' around a plant to improve the background appearance. Some photographers routinely provide a solid-colored artificial background for wildflowers. Others use a flash to darken the background and highlight the flower. Pictures can sometimes be improved in these ways, but the author prefers to minimize unnatural techniques.

For best results, especially on closeups, use a tripod for the camera. When you have the composition you like, take several pictures at different exposures to bracket the best exposure possible under the prevailing conditions.

BITTERROOT

Lewisia rediviva Pursh. The State Flower of Montana! One of the most gorgeous wildflowers in our region, now scarce in many localities. Pale pink or even white to deep rose. About 15 rounded or pointed petals overlap. The flower is 1 1/2 to 3 inches across. The blossoms appear just above ground line on short stems that rise directly from a deep root crown. Round in cross section and fleshy succulent, the leaves also grow from the root, 3/4 to 2 inches long. The leaves begin to wither before the flowers emerge in May and June, sometimes giving the impression that the plants have no life-supporting leaves. HABITAT: Dry prairies to foothill ridges, often on rocky or shallow soil. RANGE: Montana to Southern B.C., south to Colorado and California. COMMENT: Named for Capt. Meriwether Lewis, there are five species in our area and ten others west and south of our range. (See Page 54.) The Journals of Lewis and Clark note that Indians dug the roots for food, usually in the spring before they become too bitter to eat.